How to Respond to . . . SECULAR HUMANISM

Philip H. Lochhaas

THE RESPONSE SERIES
How to Respond to the Cults
How to Respond to Transcendental Meditation
How to Respond to the Lodge
How to Respond to the Latter Day Saints
How to Respond to the Occult
How to Respond to Jehovah's Witnesses
How to Respond to the Eastern Religions
How to Respond to the New Christian Religions
How to Respond to Islam
How to Respond to the Science Religions
How to Respond to Satanism
How to Respond to the New Age Movement
How to Respond to Judaism
How to Respond to Secular Humanism

Unless otherwise noted, the Scripture quotations in this publication are from The Holy Bible: NEW INTERNATIONAL VERSION, © 1973, 1978, 1984 by the International Bible Society. Used by permission of Zondervan Bible Publishers.

Humanist Manifesto quotations are from *Humanist Manifestos I and II,* © 1971 by Prometheus Books, Buffalo, NY.

Copyright © 1990 Concordia Publishing House
3558 S. Jefferson Avenue, St. Louis, MO 63118-3968
Manufactured in the United States of America

Library of Congress Cataloging-in-Publication Data

Lochhaas, Philip H., 1924-
    How to respond to—secular humanism / Philip H. Lochhaas.
      p. cm.—(The Response series)
    Includes bibliographical references.
    ISBN 0-570-04549-5
    1. Secularism—Controversial literature. 2. Humanism—
Controversial literature. 3. Apologetics—20th century.
I. Title.
BT1211.L63 1990
239'.9—dc20
                                         90-38875

1 2 3 4 5 6 7 8 9 10 PB 99 98 97 96 95 94 93 92 91

Contents

The Author

Rev. Philip H. Lochhaas is a 1948 graduate of Concordia Seminary, St. Louis, Missouri. In 1989 he retired from his position as executive secretary of the Commission on Organizations for The Lutheran Church—Missouri Synod. Prior to serving in that capacity, he was a missionary-at-large and parish pastor in Oklahoma. He received an honorary Doctor of Letters degree from Concordia Seminary in 1989.

In his position with the Commission on Organizations, Rev. Lochhaas provided thousands of inquirers annually with information and counsel regarding various religious organizations and cults. He teaches courses at Concordia Seminary on the theology of the "new religions," has written five books and numerous articles, and has lectured widely on the subject.

Foreword

Perhaps no book in the *How To Respond* series addresses so many people as this one does. Secular Humanism is a devastating philosophy because it claims that God has no place in public life—not in public education, the media, the entertainment industry, government affairs, the medical profession, business practice, nor in the host of moral and ethical decisions that touch our lives every day.

This significant work will be helpful in Bible study or discussion groups, in personal reading to understand more about the subject, and in the preparation of presentations or sermons for churches. Keep in mind two concerns as you read it:

1. Have we as churches appeared at times so "other worldly" in our message that we have come across as irrelevant and insensitive to human needs and human development? How can we become partners with leaders in the sciences and human-care professions? How can we reflect the Scriptures and help people develop the gifts and resources God has given to them?

2. Secular Humanism denies the reality of sin and its consequences, and seeks good within people. We desperately need the salvation that is found only outside ourselves in Jesus Christ. Aware of the false hopes given by Humanism, we build our hope on Christ alone.

I am sure that you will appreciate Rev. Lochhaas' book and use it to evaluate and strengthen your witness to others.

Lyle D. Muller, Executive Director
The Board for Evangelism Services
The Lutheran Church—Missouri Synod

1

Definitions

They met every Tuesday morning, fifteen to twenty ladies drawn together by a shared interest: the study of Scripture. They arrived in five or six cars, several of which they parked in their hostess' driveway and a few on the street. The women always met in the same house—until an order came from a city official: The subdivision's zoning ordinances did not permit buildings to be used as "churches" or "temples," although several neighborhood bridge clubs and the inevitable Saturday night parties were allowable. Evidently, no zoning ordinances forbade the subdivision's buildings being used for "clubhouses" or "discos."

To save a bit of postage and to add a personal touch, a young lady handed Christmas cards to her friends during her free time between high school classes. Because the cards were religious, she was ordered to cease distributing them on the school grounds because, somehow, they seemed to breach the "separation of church and state." Meanwhile, at another school, no administrator objected to posters and handbills advertising the appearance of a Buddhist monk who would explain his beliefs at the next school assembly.

Charges of violating the "separation of church and state" have been leveled in many unusual circumstances involving education:
• Against a teacher who kept a Bible on his desk along with other books he intended to read during his lunch breaks;
• Against college dormitory residents that engaged in group Bible study, although dorms had been classified as "private dwellings" in other respects;
• Against textbooks that refer to the vital role that Christian concerns have played in several of the world's major historical events;
• But not against some public secondary schools and universities that offer courses in the officially recognized and registered religion of witchcraft!

Pity the poor school principal who must administer these confusing decisions. Could the day come when it would be considered "the establishment of religion" to post in the classroom a copy of the Declaration of Independence or the fourth stanza of the national anthem, both more overtly religious than some of the items that have already been judged as violating "the separation of church and state"?

What is responsible for the arbitrary and frequently contradictory legal interpretations that serve to compound confusion rather than alleviate it? Is it true that Christianity is adversely affected while other religions pursue their ends without hindrance?

"Yes," some will insist, "and it's due to a gigantic scheme hatched by Secular Humanism." However, since humanism is not a single, clearly defined belief system but a broad philosophy with many variations and widely diverse goals, whatever is said about humanism depends on one's definition of it. To compound the issue, we need to differentiate between Secular Humanism as a specific entity and "humanism" in a general sense—neither of which can be defined to the complete satisfaction of everyone. The best we can do is to move toward a working definition.

Toward a Definition of Secular Humanism

Humanism is a pattern of thought and an attitudinal perspective rather than a specific belief system that can be defined precisely. For example, one humanist document (*Humanist Manifesto II*) declares,

> Many kinds of humanism exist in the contemporary world. The varieties and emphases of naturalistic humanism include "scientific," "democratic," "religious," and "Marxist" humanism. Free thought, atheism, agnosticism, skepticism, deism, rationalism, ethical culture and liberal religion all claim to be heirs of the humanist tradition.

Webster's dictionary offers minimal help. An earlier edition was quite specific:

> a contemporary cult of belief calling itself religious but substituting faith in man for faith in God.

Later, *Webster's Collegiate Dictionary* focused in a noncommittal way on the past:

> any system or way of thought or action concerned with the interests and ideals of people, . . . it *was* [emphasis added] characterized by an emphasis on human interests rather than the natural world or religion.

By its seventh edition, *Webster's Collegiate* returned to a more contemporary definition:

> a doctrine, attitude, or way of life centered on human interests or values; *esp.:* a philosophy that asserts the dignity and worth of man and his capacity for self-realization through reason and that often rejects supernaturalism.

Most humanists would agree to the latest definition by Webster, perhaps adding that humanists, by force of self-determination, seek to provide man with the best possible world.

For more complete information about Secular Humanism, we need to look to its spokespersons and written authorities—who do not always agree with each other. The humanist camp includes thousands of writers, lecturers, educators, and not a few hucksters. In spite of this, two documents hold center stage for humanism.

More than a half-century ago (states the preface to a recent printing of the two documents together), "a group of thirty-four liberal humanists in the United States" felt the need to create an explicit statement of the principles of Secular Humanism. The result was the publication of *A Humanist Manifesto* in 1933. Forty years later, *Humanist Manifesto II* was published to respond to admitted deficiencies in the first manifesto and to expand on its principles. The second publication was signed by "114 individuals of prominence and distinction" and "has since been endorsed by countless numbers of human beings

6

from all walks of life as a document for our time."

The manifestos' philosophy is expanded upon further and promoted in the journal *The Humanist*. The magazine, however, should not be considered a mouthpiece for all humanists, for some are quite critical of its attacks on Christianity and its intolerance of belief systems other than its own.

Our study will draw also from Marilyn Ferguson's *The Aquarian Conspiracy,* which in current literature serves as almost a bible for some Secular Humanists, in spite of the fact that Ferguson identifies herself with the New Age Movement, a movement akin to Secular Humanism but in many ways also contradictory to it. Ferguson's humanism centers in her contention that man is the sole architect of his own destiny, "a product of evolution and an instrument of evolution" (p. 412).

The Promise of Secular Humanism

Secular Humanism claims to offer hope to a world in crisis. Christians agree that the world has severe problems—in ecology, in renewable energy sources, the population crisis, world hunger, and nuclear proliferation. Also as Christians, we can say honestly that humanism's effort to address world crises is honest, sincere, and at times insightful. However, it is Secular Humanism's *religious* pronouncements that have become its most controversial and disagreeable feature for Christians.

In order to bring about its ideal world, *Human Manifesto I* proposes a new, non-theistic world "religion," a religion that *Manifesto II* describes as being based on humanity's ethical ideals, scientifically and technologically developed through faith in man's "innate potential." While we might agree with humanism's definition of religion in general as that which provides "meaning and direction, unity and purpose to human life," we cannot agree with the content of any religion that offers those benefits apart from justification by God's grace through faith in Jesus Christ.

There are many types of Secular Humanists. Therefore, we cannot consider the dedicated signers of the two manifestos to be the same as those who generally support only a few basic premises. For example, non-belief in God does not necessarily identify a person as a Secular Humanist. Nor should we consider as dedicated humanists those who have used some of its tenets as an excuse for socially irresponsible self-gratification.

Because of the maze of varying definitions of humanism (both by its opponents as well as its proponents), this book will limit its definition of Secular Humanism to that which is acknowledged by its leading spokespersons: the picture drawn in *Humanist Manifesto I* and *II,* with reference to some of its supportive literature such as the journal *The Humanist*.

2

The Humanist Manifestos

The year was 1933. It was an era of discontent brought on by the worst economic depression in the history of the United States. But with Franklin Delano Roosevelt's inauguration on March 4, 1933, the era of discontent was becoming an era of optimism. Roosevelt set a new mood for the nation as he focused on people assuming responsibility for the conditions in their country and mustering their resolve to improve their own lives.

At the time that Roosevelt was assuming the reins of government, 34 humanists were drafting their own statement, one that also called for human responsibility in solving mankind's problems: *The Humanist Manifesto*. It was based on the principle that "man is at last becoming aware that he *alone* is responsible for the world of his dreams, that he has *within himself* the power for its achievement" [emphasis added]. Man can, by his own resolve, "provide meaning and direction, unity and purpose to human life" by commitment to "reason, science, and democracy."

Although the era of optimism was interrupted by World War II, it flowered again afterward. In post-war America, a new generation of 114 humanists came to the realization that there were many areas of concern that had not been addressed by the first manifesto. Its goal: "The realization of the human potentiality of each individual and of humanity as a whole." The authors said,

> *Humanist Manifesto I,* as important as it was in its time, has since been superseded by events; though significant, it did not go far enough. It did not and could not address itself to future problems and needs. In recognition of the pressing need for a new, more relevant statement, forty years later [in 1973], *Humanist Manifesto II* was drafted. . . . [The pressing needs include] civil liberties, equality, democracy, the survival of humankind, world economic growth, population and ecological control, war and peace, . . . the building of a world community . . . the aspirations of women as well as men and people of different ethnic and racial origins.

Humanist Manifesto I

The first manifesto, barely four pages long, speaks throughout of "religious humanism," but does so under a broad definition of religion as "the means for realizing the highest values of life," adding that "religion consists of those actions, purposes, and experiences which are humanly significant." While it "does not deny the possibility of realities yet undiscovered," *Manifesto I* declares that "the nature of the universe depicted by modern science makes unacceptable any supernatural or cosmic guarantees of human values. . . . [The] religious forms and idea of our fathers [are] no longer adequate. . . . [Man] alone is responsible."

Regarding morality and ethics, *Manifesto I* says, "The goal of humanism is a free and universal society in which people voluntarily and intelligently cooperate for the common good . . . . endeavor[ing] to establish the conditions of a satisfactory life for all, not merely for the few."

Quite in contrast to the first manifesto, *Humanist Manifesto II* explicitly denies the existence of God, and it abandons the quasi-religion of *Manifesto I*. Although neither document uses the adjective "secular" to describe humanism, that meaning is proclaimed clearly in *Manifesto II*. Its formulators call themselves "non-theists" rather than atheists or agnostics because their concerns are limited to "the survival and fulfillment of the human race," a goal to which they believe God is irrelevant. As the document adds later, "We find insufficient evidence for belief in the existence of a supernatural; it is either meaningless or irrelevant to the question of the survival and fulfillment of the human race. . . . We can find no divine purpose or providence for the human species. . . . There is no credible evidence that life survives the death of the body." Since Secular Humanists accept no afterlife, the word *save* is used only in the sense of the survival of humankind in this life.

This view is consistent with the manifesto's understanding of man as material only. The existence of a human soul is an "historic concept" that has been discredited by modern science. "As far as we know, the total personality is a function of the biological organism transacting in a social and cultural context."

Only a brief section of *Humanist Manifesto II* is given directly to the topic "Ethics," but in a sense more than half the document deals with the subject. The principle is stated clearly:

> We affirm that moral values derive their source from human experience. Ethics is *autonomous* and *situational,* needing no theological or ideological sanction. Ethics stems from human need and interest. . . .
> *Reason and intelligence* are the most effective instruments that humankind possesses. . . . Critical intelligence, infused by a sense of human caring, is the best method that humanity has for resolving problems. . . . We believe in maximum individual autonomy consonant with social responsibility.

Within this ethical framework, the manifesto comments specifically on sexuality:

> While we do not approve of exploitive, denigrating forms of sexual expression, neither do we wish to prohibit, by law or social sanction, sexual behavior between consenting adults. . . . Without countenancing mindless permissiveness or unbridled promiscuity, a civilized society should be a *tolerant* one.

Since ethics is rooted in human experience alone, the manifesto also calls for the right to birth control, abortion, divorce, death with dignity, euthanasia, and even suicide.

The latter half of *Manifesto II* is a commitment to "the principles of human freedom"—participatory democracy, separation of church and state, economic well-being, elimination of all discrimination, a minimum guaranteed annual income, concern for the welfare of the disadvantaged, and the universal right to education. Believing that "decision-making must be decentralized" and that "all persons should have a voice in developing the values and goals that determine their lives," the concluding section issues a call for the "building of a world community in which all sectors of the human family can participate" in addressing the crises of war, nuclear weapons, ecology, and poverty.

The signers of the manifestos come from many walks of life. The most familiar name attached to *I* is John Dewey, the educator and philosopher who strongly influenced America's public school system. In *Manifesto II* he is joined by B. F. Skinner, Harvard's professor of psychology, whose impact on public education is equally well known. Familiar names listed among the "Additional Signers" of *II* are Joseph Fletcher of *Situational Ethics* fame; Betty Friedan, founder of the National Organization for Women (NOW); and Sir Julian Huxley, one-time head of UNESCO. Almost half of the signers are university professors. Next in number are people associated with Unitarian-Universalist churches and Ethical Culture societies. The remainder are writers, editors, businessmen, political figures, and representatives of other vocations. The list is open-ended since anyone can add his or her name by writing to *The Humanist*.

3

The Origin of Secular Humanism

Because this booklet was designed to help Christians respond to present-day Secular Humanism, only a brief sketch of the history of general humanism is given here. This chapter will demonstrate that contemporary Secular Humanism has gone far beyond all its antecedents in declaring God non-existent or, at best, irrelevant.

Textbooks in philosophy assign the beginnings of humanism to the Greek philosophers of the 5th century B.C. The Sophists, known for their clever and seemingly logical reasoning, were especially fond of quoting Protagoras (481-411 B.C.), "Man is the measure of all things." Although man was seen as the measure, some Greek philosophers nonetheless were aware of a relationship between Deity and humanity and, in spite of their devotion to reason, marveled at the mysteries in the universe. Others clearly were committed to a purely secular philosophy that prefigured the atheistic forms of humanism that later would gain ascendancy.

After the time of the New Testament church, certain Christian teachers attempted to harmonize the Greek preoccupation with human reason with Christian teachings concerning the deity of Jesus Christ. In so doing, they hoped to make Christianity more palatable to potential converts in the Greek world—but in fact they did violence to Scripture and were responsible for some of the most destructive heresies ever to trouble the Christian church. The authors of these heresies, however, unwittingly moved teachers faithful to the Scriptures to prepare explicit confessions of faith still treasured by orthodox believers today: the Nicene and Athanasian Creeds.

During the period referred to as the Dark Ages (A.D. 476-1450), human reason continued to be elevated. Thomas Aquinas (c. 1225-74) was prominent among the Italian humanists who developed "natural theology," the teaching that man's intellect by itself could lead him to divine truth. Aquinas admitted that some Christian mysteries were indeed above reason, but he insisted that they were not contradictory to it. He believed that man's *will* opposed God, but he reserved man's intellect from such opposition, holding that the intellect was not included in man's total depravity caused by the fall into sin. Some of Aquinas' followers carried his ideas even farther by teaching that man still retains a measure of the perfection in which he was created, thus laying the groundwork for the philosophy developed during the Renaissance (14th—16th centuries) when expressions of humanism insisted on "an innate goodness in man."

The Lutheran Reformation of the 16th century returned the Bible to its place as the only unimpeachable authority in religion, and committed itself to "Scripture alone."

During the post-Reformation period, reason again was enthroned; and with the so-called "Age of Enlightenment" (18th century), science was elevated to the position of final authority—thus smoothing the transition to Deism (19th century). The Deists affirmed that reason supports the existence of God, but they rejected all divine revelation and authority. Much of what the Deists wrote was negative and attacked Christian doctrine—both divine revelation as well as the concept of absolute truth. Once man was persuaded that he could be sure of nothing, a new "Age of Skepticism" was born, culminating in overt atheism and, eventually, the complete replacement of God with man. It is this final step of man usurping God's throne that distinguishes the Secular Humanism of the 20th century from earlier forms of general humanism.

The Making of a Secular Humanist

For a complete understanding of the origin of Secular Humanism, it is necessary to go farther back, back before the golden age of Greek philosophy, back to man's own origin.

When God created Adam and Eve to inhabit the earth and tend it, an intimate relationship existed between them and God. They enjoyed fellowship with God and obeyed his good and gracious will. God walked "in the garden in the cool of the day" (Gen. 3:8), to be with and talk with Adam and Eve; yet his authority was to be unquestioned and as absolute as it had been when he spoke the creative word "Let there be . . . and there was" (Gen. 1, *passim).*

That which destroyed man's relationship with God might well be called the first faint whispering of humanism—followed by a blatant declaration such as a thoroughgoing Secular Humanist might make today. Satan, the Prince of Darkness, breathed into the ear of the "mother of all the living" (Gen. 3:20) and spoke the first suggestion of Secular Humanism: "Did God really say . . .?" followed with the unconscionable lie, "You will be like God" (Gen. 3:1-5). From Eve to her husband and through them to all generations the lie was told: *Independence from the Creator is the glory of man. Disobeying God brings happiness and fulfillment.*

Immediately the futility of their choice became evident in the guilt and shame which they had not known before. Anger and hatred were born, in turn giving way to violence and murder. In place of communion with God, hatred of God became the natural state of man. "The mind of sinful man is death . . . the sinful mind is hostile to God. It does not submit to God's law, nor can it do so. Those controlled by the sinful nature cannot please God" (Rom. 8:6-8). And the wicked are recorded as asking, "How can God know? Does the Most High have knowledge?" (Ps. 73:11); "What does God know? . . . Thick clouds veil him, so he does not see us" (Job 22:13-14).

Thus, through Adam and Eve, we all became both the perpetrators and the victims of our sad bid for independence from our Creator. It appeared to be only a hint of evil at first; yet it is but a small step from rejecting the absolute authority of God to questioning whether he has any authority at all—or even if he exists!

Not all denials of God's existence are as vitriolic as those of Madalyn Murray O'Hair's *American Atheists;* some denials (such as in *Human Manifesto II*) simply define God out of the picture. The view is not a 20th century innovation. "In his pride the wicked man does not seek [God]; in all his thoughts there is no room for God" (Ps. 10:4). "The fool says in his heart, 'There is no God' " (Ps. 14:1). With a "hollow and deceptive philosophy" (Col. 2:8), the Secular Humanist knows no god but himself—and, as a result, has no guide

12

through the dark night of his own soul. His greatest boast is a whistling in the dark: "He says to himself, 'Nothing will shake me; I'll always be happy and never have trouble' " (Ps. 10:6). Secular Humanism may believe that when we have developed our full potential, all our crises will be overcome; but all sacred and human history tears off the mask of that assertion. Nevertheless, it is crucial for the Secular Humanist to have such faith in humanity because he has no faith in God; without faith in humanity, he would be left only with despair.

From denial of God's authority, to denial of his existence, to enthronement of man in place of God: these are the steps of becoming a Secular Humanist. To put it another way, the logical progression from Satan's lies, from "Did God really say" to "You will be like God," is both the origin and the history of Secular Humanism.

> Sad little man, strutting on his dung-heap and crowing defiantly at the sun as it rises, and often believing that without his crow the sun would not come up at all!
>
> Taylor Caldwell, *Dialogues with the Devil*

4

Secular Humanism:
The Dehumanization of Man

To some degree, Christianity and Secular Humanism appear to have much the same goal for life in this world:

> If the starting point of humanism is the preservation and enhancement of all things human, then what more worthwhile goal than the realization of the human potentiality of each individual and of humanity as a whole? . . . [Humanist Manifesto II is] committed to both human fulfillment and survival. . . . Humanists are committed to building a world that is significant, not only for the individual's quest for meaning, but for the whole of humankind. (Preface)

> The Preciousness and dignity of the individual person is a central humanist value. . . . [Also] We urge recognition of the common humanity of all people. We further urge the use of reason and compassion to produce the kind of world we want—a world in which peace, prosperity, freedom, and happiness are widely shared . . . [a goal that requires] commitment to all humankind. . . . (Humanist Manifesto II)

The manifestos describe themselves as a call, "a vision of hope, a direction for satisfying survival." The basic rationale seems to be that, based on the inherent worth of every individual, a system of ethics can be developed which will enhance that worth so that all humanity can live in peace, prosperity, and freedom.

Developing the necessary system of ethics and morals, however, has been a problem for Secular Humanism. Consider the following statements, written about two years apart:

> [W]e shall find it no easy task to mold a natural ethic strong enough to maintain moral restraint and social order without the supernatural consolations, hopes and fears. There is no significant example in history, before our time, of a society successfully maintaining moral life without the aid of religion. (The Humanist, Feb. 1977, p. 26]

> Julian Huxley . . . [American Humanist Association] Humanist of the year in 1962, "thought it possible to establish a moral system which would be purely scientific in inspiration and which would be capable of uniting mankind." But the humanist movement that Huxley projected has made only limited progress toward such a morality . . . and we are still far from united on a number of basic questions . . . and there's little hope of uniting the movement, let alone the world unless we find a way to fuller consensus. (The Humanist, March/April, 1979, p. 41)

While Secular Humanists would reject the conclusion, the reason they haven't been able to find such an ethic is that they have not built their system on the true value of all individuals as God's creatures. Instead, they view man as the measure of all things who must save himself, and as having the power to achieve his dreams. This view *dehumanizes* people instead of empowering them for morality.

Denial of the Worth and Dignity of Man

Secular Humanism's dehumanization of man begins by repudiating man's dignity as a special creation of God. It dismisses God as non-existent or, at most, "meaningless and irrelevant to the question of the survival and fulfillment of the human race." In fact, it says, "False 'theologies of hope' and messianic ideologies ... cannot cope with existing world realities." Humanity merely "has emerged as a result of a continuous process ... [with] no uniquely religious emotions and attitudes hitherto associated with belief in the supernatural" and that "the human species is an emergence from natural evolutionary forces" with no possibility of an afterlife. Therefore, to the question "what is man?" Secular Humanism answers, *we are animals*. It has not answered, of course, how a mere animal, a "self-existent" collection of molecules, a "biological organism," can manufacture hopes and fears, loves and beliefs, standards of right and wrong, and lofty goals in life. *Manifesto II* can state only that "the total personality is a function of the biological organism transacting in a social and cultural context." Therefore, all attempts by Secular Humanism to define good and evil can be no more than descriptions of what is taking place among accidental biological combinations. Objective morality does not exist.

The critical question to be raised, however, is whether humanity, on its own, ever will be able to develop the ethics, morals, and values which Secular Humanism admits are necessary. In fact, it cannot.

Secular Humanism contains an inherent contradiction. How, for example, does the right to abortion, euthanasia, and suicide square with the "preciousness and dignity of the individual person," "full realization of human potential," and "the good life here and now"? Or, compare the Humanist rights of one individual over against another. How can the right to "the many varieties of sexual exploration" be lived out "short of harming others" when great harm is done to spouses, children, whole professions, and entire communities by the actions of "consenting adults"? No lifestyle is ever completely private; it always has an effect for good or evil on the whole moral climate of the society.

Without actually putting it into words, the goal of Secular Humanism is the supremacy of individual self-gratification. Even those who wish to extend the goal beyond the individual cannot go beyond communal self-interest (not even when the community is defined as humanity as a whole). The reason is that, for Secular Humanism, nothing exists beyond or above humanity in the here and now.

Self-gratification and self-interest have never brought about the kind of world envisioned by Secular Humanism. Instead, they bring about the stuff of headlines. They reinforce repressive, totalitarian societies. They breed anarchy, especially in poverty.

Still, the Christian cannot accuse every Humanist of being amoral or immoral (or accuse every immoral or amoral person as being a Secular Humanist). Quite the contrary.

> Moral obligations are factual in character, as factual as debts at the bank, usually accompanied by feelings of the heart, but completely independent of those feelings or lack of them. We owe, whether we like it or not. And people who are ready to come to terms with the facts should have as little trouble in agreeing about the wrong of murder and slavery and dishonesty and double-

cross as scientists do in agreeing about the law of gravitation. (*The Humanist,* March/April, 1979, p.44)

I believe that people can solve their problems by using imagination and common sense applied with courage and following basic moral principles. (*The Humanist,* January/February 1980, p. 41)

Without realizing it, the authors of these quotes are edging toward the truth. There *are* moral obligations that are factual apart from human feelings. There *are* basic moral principles. They *are* just as real as the law of gravitation. And they *do* exist within the hearts of us all, Secular Humanists included, because God placed them there.

When Gentiles, who do not have the law, do by nature things required by the law, they are a law for themselves, even though they do not have the law, since they show that the requirements of the law are written on their hearts, their consciences also bearing witness, and their thoughts now accusing, now even defending them (Rom. 2:14-15).

Even so, consciences are dulled by the effects of sin. That's why even the most humanly altruistic sense of communal good is still self-interest, still gratification delayed but a step farther. Christians might well worry about how long a society built on explicit Biblical values, morals, and ethics can expect to survive the systematic attacks of a small but vociferous group of key Secular Humanists in the national education system, entertainment, and news media.

True Humanism

The dictionary says "worth" is determined by either of two ways: 1) by intrinsic value or merit; or 2) by the esteem in which a person or thing is held by another, the price that another is willing to pay to possess something.

Secular Humanism would like to believe that it truly is human because it uplifts the value of man. In fact, however, Secular Humanism gives mankind no worth or dignity (dignity defined as "the quality or state of being worthy, honored, or esteemed"). We have no more intrinsic value than any animal; and the only esteem between people is that which eventually will gratify the self.

In contrast to Secular Humanism's empty assertion, Christianity can claim to be the true humanism which truly espouses the worth and dignity of mankind and of each individual.

1. *True humanism begins with the definition of man as that given by the Maker of man:*

"You [God] made him a little lower than the heavenly beings and crowned him with glory and honor. You made him ruler over the works of your hands; you put everything under his feet" (Ps. 8:5-6).
God saw all that he had made, and it was very good (Gen. 1:31).

It is not what man is made of that makes him valuable, but the fact that he was fashioned in the image of God and given life by God himself:

The Lord God formed the man from the dust of the ground and breathed into his nostrils the breath of life, and the man became a living being (Gen. 2:7).

2. *True humanism also begins with a realistic admission of mankind's current situation:*

The manifestos barely acknowledge that the moral and ethical life of man-

16

kind has not reached "the complete realization of human personality." And after pointing out a list of abuses (including Nazism and other totalitarian regimes, science's own evil results, inhuman wars, and police states), the Preface to *Manifesto II* calls us to "an affirmative and hopeful vision, . . . [to] faith . . ." in order to choose properly "between despair and hope." Secular Humanism, however, cannot admit that which is so obvious, that evil is more than an occasional outbreak; evil permeates every human.

> They are corrupt, their deeds are vile; there is no one who does good. The Lord looks down from heaven on the sons of men to see if there are any who understand, any who seek God. All have turned aside, they have together become corrupt; there is no one who does good, not even one. (Ps. 14:1b-3)

A view from the earth reveals the same as one from heaven: mankind does not live by even its own weak morality. Evil thoughts, sexual immorality, theft, murder, adultery, greed, malice, deceit, lewdness, envy, slander, arrogance, folly—they all permeate society because, as Mark 7:21 points out, they come from man's heart, from his very being. Man is "by nature sinful and unclean."

Secular Humanism responds to the pervasiveness of evil with two assertions: 1. Man in himself has the resources to overcome evil; and 2. Evil has no eternal significance.

The first of these two assumptions requires a large leap of faith on the part of Secular Humanists. Not even the most idealistic psychiatrist, psychologist, sociologist, or scientist can point to an individual who has totally overcome innate self-centered self-interest in order to serve the good of others. The honest Secular Humanist will agree with Christianity in concluding that people can "progress" in moral/ethical living but will never achieve anything resembling perfection. How could it be otherwise? The natural heart that produces only evil cannot devise an ethical system that will produce a truly moral society.

The second assumption, that evil has no eternal significance, contradicts the testimony of the human conscience that evil is a sin against God, a sin which provokes his anger. While the existence of a God who holds mankind responsible for the evil in its heart cannot be proven scientifically, its truth is obvious. As the apostle Paul pointed out,

> [W]hat may be known about God is plain to them, because God has made it plain to them, for since the creation of the world God's invisible qualities—his eternal power and divine nature—have been clearly seen, being understood from what has been made, so that men are without excuse (Rom. 1:19-20).

Therefore, true humanism, seeing the current situation as it really is, includes accountability to God for sin. In reality, sin is the problem behind all the crises of the world.

3. *True humanism offers the only solution to man's innate and worldwide problem of sin:*

God has rescued humanity by means of his only-begotten Son, Jesus Christ. Human philosophy can sink into despair over the hopeless human condition, or it can ignore the true condition and blithely anticipate the day when humanity creates its own heaven on earth (the view of Secular Humanism)—but human philosophy cannot deal with both the problem and the solution.

For the Secular Humanist, the truth of the pervasiveness of sin is repugnant because it removes the possibility of man building a truly moral society.

If people had the ability to overcome absolutely the evil in their own hearts, then they could save themselves (as the manifestos say they should). Satan's first question to man, "Did God really say . . ." and first promise, "You will be like God . . ." (Gen. 3:1,5) still plague us all.

Secular Humanism has rejected "salvationism" as a solution because of what it sees as the failure of religion and the Christian church in particular.

> Salvationism, based on mere affirmation, still appears as harmful, diverting people with false hopes of heaven hereafter. (*II*)

> [T]raditional dogmatic or authoritarian religions that place revelation, God, ritual, or creed above human needs and experience do a disservice to the human species. (*II*)

> Traditional religions often offer solace to humans, but, as often, they inhibit humans from helping themselves or experiencing their full potential. Such institutions, creeds, and rituals often impede the will to serve others. Too often traditional faiths encourage dependence rather than independence, obedience rather than affirmation, fear rather than courage. (*II*)

Just as Secular Humanism is unable to see the sinful nature behind the facade of "ideal man," so it has not seen the truth of the Gospel. We must admit that Christianity cannot produce a perfect society on earth, and its belief in an afterlife is not intended as an escape from responsibility in the here and now. But the truth is that, in spite of the knowledge of God and his absolute law, the sinful nature of man has corrupted every human heart and infects every social situation—and, therefore, we are responsible and accountable. Since the solution cannot come from within us, we have nowhere to turn but to God.

> When I want to do good, evil is right there with me. For in my inner being I delight in God's law; but I see another law at work in the members of my body, waging war against the law of my mind and making me a prisoner of the law of sin at work within my members. What a wretched man I am! Who will rescue me from this body of death? Thanks be to God—through Jesus Christ our Lord! (Rom. 7:21-25).

Man's sinful nature, however, does not rule out man's ultimate value. Rather, it points us to the second definition of "worth": it is determined by the esteem in which a person or thing is held by another, the price that another is willing to pay to possess something. Even though that worth is not measurable by human science, its truth is established by him who made and loved us so much that, in spite of our sin, "he gave his one and only Son, that whoever believes in him should not perish but have eternal life" (John 3:16). God showed how much he values humankind by paying the price of his own Son to redeem all people.

This truth is scorned by Secular Humanism because it is beyond all human understanding. In an article in *The Humanist* (January/February, 1979, p. 5), the writer describes those who "contract the condition called 'knowing Jesus' or something analogous thereto" as having an "incorrigible world view, . . . immune to education and incurable, . . . truly sophomoric, half-sophisticated and half-moronic." The Bible anticipates such opposition. "The message of the cross is foolishness to those who are perishing. . . . For the foolishness of God is wiser than man's wisdom, and the weakness of God is stronger than man's strength" (1 Cor. 1:18–25).

4. *True humanism knows that by God's grace some people have far surpassed that which would be possible by human effort alone.*

Only God's grace in Jesus Christ enables people to achieve their true potential, the purpose for which God created them. For the story of man's potential as it is re-created by the Spirit of God, read the whole of Hebrews 11 and the exhortation following in 12:1-3:

> Therefore, since we are surrounded by such a great cloud of witnesses, let us throw off everything that hinders and the sin that so easily entangles, and let us run with perseverance the race marked out for us. Let us fix our eyes on Jesus, the author and perfecter of our faith . . . Consider him . . . so that you do not grow weary and lose heart.

All in all, Secular Humanism selected an appropriate name for itself to reflect its assumption that people can become ideally humane without God. Sad to say, it actually *de*humanizes people because it denies their true human condition and points to a solution that cannot work. God has correctly defined us as a special creation of his that he loves dearly. However, since the fall we are by nature sinful and unclean and unable to save ourselves. But God offers us a renewed intimate relationship with him through his Son's death and resurrection—a relationship in which he alone makes possible the truly humane life, the sanctified life described, for example, in the Beatitudes and in Gal. 5:22-23.

5

The Spread of Secular Humanism

Without question, the influence of Secular Humanism is growing—often subtly and insidiously. It happens when

- a newsperson inserts Secular Humanist editorial opinion into news reporting;
- a political program redefines rights established by the Constitution in a way that hinders witness to any faith other than Secular Humanism;
- a scientist declares as "fact" that which is not scientific because it is unproven, not reproducible, or self-contradictory;
- a humanistic psychologist operates from the assumption expressed in *Humanist Manifesto II,* that ". . . science can account for the causes of behavior."

Of course, not all those who espouse Secular Humanist ideas would call themselves Secular Humanists. The spread of Secular Humanism, therefore, cannot be mapped adequately; it is a philosophy (even a kind of religion), not an organization. However, to understand its spread across the United States, we here look at the broad acceptance of just two comparatively new slogans influencing the country, "the separation of church and state" and "individual autonomy."

The Use of Slogans

1. The Separation of Church and State

Many Americans are not aware that "separation" is not a constitutional provision but a phrase Thomas Jefferson used in a letter to defend himself against the accusation of being an infidel. There is no reason to believe that the founding fathers intended to divorce religion from the state. Many of them sought divine guidance every step of the way in forming the new nation. However, since 1947, Jefferson's phrase has been popularized as a slogan by those who attempt to make it appear that Secular Humanism was the ideal for which the founding fathers strove.

Compare the tenet of "separation of church and state" to the following resolution at the Constitutional Convention in Philadelphia, June 28, 1787, suggested by Benjamin Franklin:

> I have lived, sir, a long time, and the longer I live, the more convincing proof I see of this truth—that God governs in the affairs of men. And if a sparrow cannot fall to the ground without His notice, is it probable that an empire can rise without His aid? We have been assured, sir, in the sacred writings, "that except the Lord build the house, they labor in vain that build it" (Ps. 127:1). I firmly believe this; and I also believe that without His concurring aid we shall succeed in this political building no better than the builders of Babel. I therefore beg leave to move, That henceforth prayers imploring the assistance of Heaven and its blessing on our deliberations be held in this assembly every morning before we proceed to business.

Although Franklin's motion was not acted upon, it delineated a truth that already had been enunciated by Jefferson in the Declaration of Independence, that "all men are created equal, that they are endowed by their Creator with certain unalienable rights." These rights are "unalienable" because they are derived from an authority higher than man. That alone is sufficient reason to hold all men, individually and in society, accountable to God for their actions in society.

This rationale for independence also became the foundation of United States constitutional law. Whether deist or Christian by profession, the men who forged the Declaration and the Constitution agreed that all men, the governor and the governed alike, are under the law of God. For the framers of these documents, moral decisions must be made according to standards which are both divine and absolute.

Almost concurrently with the Constitution (separated by only 15 months), ten amendments were proposed, known as the Bill of Rights. The first of these declares that "Congress shall make no law respecting the establishment of religion or prohibiting the free exercise thereof." This amendment, adopted for the protection of both church and state, does not mandate the *separation* of religion and state. (Nor does any other provision in the Constitution.) There is a world of difference between recognition of the Creator-God and specific creeds or acts of worship. The founding fathers heartily agreed that responsibility to God is the foundation of law, but they would not tolerate governmental requiring, supporting, or favoring one religious creed to the exclusion of another.

Having said this, we do not argue that the government should require belief in Christianity or any other religion. Just as we would be appalled to be required to acknowledge as true or participate in non-Christian worship or thought, so we could not accept a state-driven Christianity forced on others. But no political decision can ever negate God's existence or his special creation of man as a being with God-given "unalienable" rights, responsible to him.

Therefore, the Secular Humanist implication that citizens should divorce faith from civil decisions is a recent innovation and not the intention of the Constitution.

2. Individual Autonomy

Similar to the separation of church and state, the Secular Humanists push for "individual autonomy" is modifying the basic belief of social responsibility and accountability under God. While some would claim that the worst abuses of the "Me Generation" have been laid aside, its age-old hallmarks continue to spread among the general population:

Striving for instant gratification;
Individualism at the expense of fellow men; and
Egocentric materialism at the expense of community welfare.

Each of these desensitizes people so that they no longer feel accountable for their actions, and thus they contribute to a sharp decline in the morals of society.

True, when *Humanist Manifesto II* declares, "We believe in maximum individual autonomy consonant with social responsibility," it appears to stand in opposition to the philosophy of total selfishness. And some of the "social responsibility" statements of the manifesto do speak against an unrestricted selfishness, particularly those that promote the good of all (not just "the favored

21

few") and decry the "debasing forces of vulgarization, commercialization, bureaucratization, and dehumanization."

Too many people, however, ignore the statements on responsibility and focus instead on the "right" to establish one's own moral standards without regard for how these standards may affect others. *Manifesto II* maintains that "private" acts must not impinge on the rights of others, but few if any of the "private" choices described in the document are even remotely private—they affect deeply the moral standards, expectancies, rights, health, choices, and even the lives of other human beings. Consider some of the "autonomous" slogans of today:

- "A woman should have power over her own body and should not be accountable to anyone else"—thus justifying universal abortion on demand.
- "Whatever happens between consenting adults is no one's business but their own"—releasing a host of perversions upon all of society, bringing about a climate of debased morals that affects all.
- "Adults should be permitted to choose for themselves what they would like to see and hear"—the rationale behind the flood of pornography and obscenity that assaults the eyes of children as well as adults who do not wish to "see and hear" but cannot escape the societal saturation of these things.

These are but a few illustrations of how quickly autonomy can lead toward anarchy when accountability to God is disassociated from the actions of men.

Avenues of Entry for Secular Humanism

1. The Entertainment Industry

Outside of the educational system (see below), Secular Humanism has found the entertainment industry a most powerful ally in spreading its philosophy. Movies, television, and even the comic strips frequently make Christian moral standards the butt of jokes. Living above the law is often portrayed as the good life. The god to be worshiped is the freedom to do, say, or promote whatever one pleases. Consider also contemporary music and its constant repetition of the themes "do your own thing" and "don't let anyone tell you"—holding up humanist ideals to the most inexperienced and impressionable segment of society.

2. The Public Education System

In order to become the religion of the next century, Secular Humanism must counteract the effects of the primary transmitter of cultural and religious values: the family. The most productive route for that is the school system—illustrated by a brash statement made by Dr. C. M. Pierce of Harvard University at a childhood education seminar in 1973. (The content was reaffirmed in 1983 in a telephone conversation with Caryl Matrisciana [*Gods of the New Age,* p. 170]).

> Every child in America entering school at the age of five is mentally ill, because he comes to school with certain allegiances toward our founding fathers, toward our elected officials, toward his parents, toward belief in a supernatural Being, toward the sovereignty of this nation as a separate entity. It's up to you teachers to make all these sick children well by creating the international children of the future.

About the same time, Secular Humanist John Dunphy emphasized a similar point in *The Humanist* journal (January/February 1983, p. 26; emphasis added):

I am convinced that the battle for humankind's future must be waged and won in the public school classrooms by teachers who correctly perceive their role as the proselyters of a new faith, a religion of humanity. These teachers must embody the same selfless dedication as the most rabid fundamentalist preachers, for they will be ministers of another sort, utilizing a classroom instead of a pulpit to convey humanist values *in whatever subject they teach,* regardless of the educational level—*preschool day care to large state university* . . . the classroom must and will become an arena of conflict between the old and the new—the rotting corpse of Christianity, together with all its adjacent evils and misery, and the new faith of Humanism, resplendent in its promise of a world in which the never-realized Christian idea of 'Love thy neighbor' will finally be achieved.

And Marilyn Ferguson—futurist, educator, spellbinding lecturer, and producer of the bi-weekly *Brain/Mind Bulletin*—affirms in her book *The Aquarian Conspiracy* (p. 280), "You can have a new society, the visionaries have said, if you change the education of the younger generation."

Public education is by far the single greatest source of Secular Humanist influence in society today because it impacts such a large number of people at their most impressionable age. There is no greater opportunity for mass indoctrination than that which is afforded by the public school at every educational level.

While the outsider can hardly say that somewhere a group of avowed Secular Humanist generals is sitting in a back room plotting a formal attack on religion and the family, it is true that in the area of education many Secular Humanists *are* building a strong coalition.

Ferguson boasts, "Of the Aquarian Conspirators surveyed, more were involved in education than in any other single category of work. They were teachers, administrators, policy makers, educational psychologists . . . tens of thousands . . . and faculty members in colleges of education . . . among the millions engaged in *personal transformation*" (pp. 180-281). At the same time, however, Ferguson warns that "their efforts [are] too often thwarted by peers, administrators, parents." Therefore she counts among her heroes Mario Fantini, "former Ford consultant on education, now at the State University of New York," whom she quotes as saying, "The psychology of becoming has to be smuggled into the schools" (p. 281). Ferguson also quotes Dr. Beverly Galyean (d. 1984), curriculum developer for the Los Angeles city schools and Secular Humanist, as saying, "The crises [in discipline, learning, attendance, etc.] now facing most school districts can be the springboard for your own humanist experiments" (p. 314). This comes from a curriculum developer who wrote elsewhere of "reowning the Godlikeness within us" and of the human potential for "perfect love . . . perfect wisdom . . . [and] perfect understanding."

Ferguson, a strong proponent of man's potential for continuing evolution toward perfection, is trying zealously to unite all voices that promote the doctrine of unlimited human potential. However, she causes some consternation among secular humanists of a more "purist" persuasion on two counts: 1) in her zeal she embraces the whole "New Age" spiritualized version of humanism, from the seriously religious to the silly; and 2) she employs a common propaganda device called bifurcation. She sets up "paradigms" in which everything she perceives as "good" is credited to the human-potential movement, and everything detrimental is blamed on "the old way of doing things."

In spite of Furgeson's problems, her appeal and efforts for a united push of Secular Humanism in education is being heard—because it seems to meet a need. Parents and educators across the country are greatly alarmed over the lack of moral training given children and youth and over their consequent irresponsibility for their behavior. The situation has become so desperate that administrators and classroom teachers (including some in private schools) reach for any program that promises help. As a result, humanistic philosophy, itself responsible for much of the decline in morals, can through special programs become deeply entrenched in the classroom without parents or teachers recognizing it.

One of those "special programs" is a specific kind of "values clarification." Please note the limiting words, "a specific kind." In a general sense, everyone clarifies values whenever they make choices. The process measures alternatives—their advantages, their costs, their consequences, their effect on others— according to one's standard, which for most people is reliable and fixed according to an objective given (for Christians, the standard is God). Values clarification in Secular Humanism has no such standard. In its place are feelings, situational circumstances, subjective preferences, and all too often the popular opinion of inexperienced peers.

Secular Humanists argue that external standards are unnecessary because the human being, especially the child, is innately good and will arrive at the right choice quite naturally. Even more than innately good, the human being is seen as "godlike" by nature, unlimited in potential, and capable of progressive evolution. *Education* is seen as the key to unlocking the unlimited potential.

Although secular humanism's goal of improving the human condition may be noble and sincere, the dream will fare no better than that of the builders of the Tower of Babel if the reality of a Creator-God to whom all are responsible is denied. Such was the conviction of the founding fathers—and the foundation upon which the United States Constitution was built.

6

A Christian Response to Secular Humanism

At most, only a few hundred thousand people in the land consider themselves "card-carrying" Secular Humanists. These, together with their committed followers, make up a very small fraction of the total population. However, their influence extends much further than their numbers suggest, for many of them occupy key positions in high-visibility fields such as the entertainment industry, the news media, government, and publishing. Their philosophy often is absorbed unconsciously because many people are unprepared to recognize it.

Christians need not sit idly by while Satan urges people to ignore or deny the existence of God. We have an obligation to all people and to God to proclaim the *whole* truth—the truth of sin and grace—not just that which is thought to be "scientific." How we do that is grouped here under four themes: Awareness; Compassion; Action; and Witness.

Awareness

In order to combat the encroachment of Secular Humanism, we need to (1) be aware of what it is and how it is spreading, and (2) help others, Christians and non-Christians alike, understand what it is and how it compares to God's Truth. We restate here the basics as detailed in previous chapters.

At the heart of Secular Humanism (as distinct from the New Age Movement) stands the assumption that the physical life is all there is.

> We find insufficient evidence for belief in the existence of a supernatural; it is either meaningless or irrelevant to the question of the survival and fulfillment of the human race. . . . [W]e must save ourselves. (*II*)

Man's life, however, is not intended to be lived on a flat, one-dimensional plane; it has a vertical dimension as well as a horizontal one: Both dimensions are maintained by the Creator through the redemption and restoration that is in the Savior Jesus Christ. Neither relationship can be abrogated merely by rebelling against it; but denial of responsibility does doom man to experiencing only a one-dimensional life devoid of "love, joy, peace, patience, kindness, goodness, faithfulness, gentleness and self-control" (Gal. 5:22) as well as all else that "God has prepared for those who love him" (1 Cor. 2:9).

We need the vertical dimension in order to deal with *all* the issues and problems of life: social, environmental, educational, industrial, commercial, political, artistic, medical, agricultural, and communicative—every field of human endeavor. Man and his achievements are never the center of the Christian's devotion. That is reserved for the Savior-God who is man's Source of Life and who has given man his identity and worth in Jesus Christ.

Aware of the vertical dimension of human life, the Christian can use profitably a number of methodologies otherwise despoiled apart from God. For example, in the light of man's vertical relationship to God, "Values Clarification" becomes a valid concept. The vertical dimension provides both a definition and a standard of measurement.

He [God] has showed you, O man, what is good. And what does the Lord require of you? To act justly and to love mercy and to walk humbly with your God" (Micah 6:8).

"Behavior Modification," too, is a valid concept when it is in a vertical relationship with God; it can describe Christian sanctification. The "Modifier" is the Holy Spirit of God, who by Word and Sacrament continually cleanses and renews the Christian's behavior and empowers the Christian man and woman to grow in service to God and fellow-man.

In Christ Jesus ... whatever is true, whatever is noble, whatever is right, whatever is pure, whatever is lovely, whatever is admirable—if anything is excellent and praiseworthy—think about such things ... And the God of peace will be with you" (Phil. 4:7-9).

Even the goal of "self-realization" takes on validity when it is considered in the light of man's vertical relationship to God. An honest realization of "self" acknowledges humanity's dependence on God for life and all that belongs to the needs of life—including a moral standard by which human beings can live without preying on and destroying one another. Above all, valid self-realization cherishes the special worth, the dignity, that God has placed on man through the blood of Jesus Christ shed to cleanse man from sin.

In summary, Christians need to be able to identify Secular Humanism, but they also need to be able to help the "searching person" be aware of and believe in the ideal humanism provided by God in Christ Jesus.

Compassion

Compassion should mark the Christian's demeanor. A cue must be taken from the Savior who, "when he saw the crowds, had compassion on them because they were harassed and helpless, like sheep without a shepherd" (Matt. 9:36). In reality, some Christians overzealously condemn everyone who happens to express a Secular Humanist point of view. They say in effect, "All humanists attack their parents and the church. They believe in suicide, abortion, licentiousness, adultery, sexual perversion, lying, stealing, killing, etc."

The condemnation employs a common and unbecoming propaganda device called "the sweeping generalization." True, some Secular Humanists (including the manifestos) quite blatantly and unconditionally defend some of those items and approve of others under special circumstances—but some Secular Humanists would approve of none of them. Many Secular Humanists, with high moral standards derived in the main from their Judeo-Christian heritage, sincerely are concerned about the widespread lack of personal responsibility, rampant immorality, crime, violence, hunger, disease, and war. For many sincere seekers, Secular Humanism is a haven because they do not know where else to go. Because they have been led to believe that Secular Humanism alone is concerned with and has the solution for mankind's condition, it is the philosophy with which they identify. These people are victims of false information who deserve the Christian's compassion, "speaking the truth in love" (Eph. 4:15).

Keep yourselves in God's love as you wait for the mercy of our Lord Jesus Christ to bring you to eternal life. Be merciful to those who doubt; snatch others from the fire and save them; to others show mercy mixed with fear . . . . (Jude 21-23)

Love translated into action is the course that the Lord lays out for the Christian.

Action

Mere avoidance of the influences of Secular Humanism does not fully discharge the Christian's obligation to truth. Compassion requires the action of "speaking the truth in love" (Eph. 4:15): reaching out with the love of Jesus Christ to those who are unaware that their responsibility is to God as well as fellow man. Such action begins with prayer—acknowledging and requesting God's help, trusting that prayers in accord with the will of God will be answered (Matt. 7:8).

> I urge, then, first of all, that requests, prayers, intercession, and thanksgiving be made for everyone—for kings and for all those in authority, that we may lead peaceful and quiet lives in all godliness and holiness. This is good, and pleases God our Savior, who wants all men to be saved and to come to a knowledge of the truth" (1 Tim. 2:1-4).

Such fervent prayer not only affirms the ultimate and gracious governance of God in the affairs of men, but is "powerful and effective" (James 5:16) in bringing God's healing power to bear on the discharge of governmental responsibilities. Having thus prayed for responsibility to God on the part of those who are in positions of influence, Christians individually and collectively must ask themselves, "What will we do to declare the truth of God in our 1) homes, 2) churches, 3) classrooms, and 4) community?"

1. The Home and Family

In spite of present-day advocacy of "alternate lifestyles," (living together outside of marriage, conditional or temporary arrangements, same-sex "marriages," polygamy, etc.), the nuclear family (committed father, mother, and children) is the basic unit of society and the only family lifestyle directly instituted by God and promised His blessing (Gen. 2:18-24 and Eph. 6:1-3). Every concerned citizen, and especially every Christian citizen, must address the task of preserving the family structure in our society.

Families living in Christ can close the door to those Secular Humanist influences that belittle God's moral standards and attempt to change the family shape. Such influences include the materialistic standards by which social status is measured: the kind of heroes or villians that are depicted on television as well as in music, magazines, novels, and even some newspapers; and especially the "cheap-shot" comedians and talk-show hosts who entertain audiences by ridiculing Christian values. When such Secular Humanist messages cannot be kept out of the family, they can be analyzed and evaluated for what they are and rejected. Families who do this understand that they form the first line of defense against Secular Humanist forces that would trade away genuine freedom under God for a false "independence" from God that is rooted in human fallibility and impotence. These families are sustained and, even more, empowered by the Spirit of God through study of the Word, regular worship, use of the Sacraments and prayer. They bring strength, joy, peace, and hope to all whose lives they touch.

2. The Church

Next to the family, the church as an institution is most vulnerable to the invasion of humanist philosophy. In reality, the church is men and women who are "called to be saints" (Rom. 1:7), "strong in the Lord" (Eph. 6:10), not "blown here and there by every wind of teaching and by the cunning and craftiness of men in their deceitful scheming" (Eph. 4:14) or by "men who divide you, who follow mere natural instincts and do not have the Spirit" (Jude 19).

But because of the current decline in overall church membership and attendance, some churches have concluded that they are failing to be "relevant" to a society whose values and standards change rapidly and often unpredictably. Listening to the questions of Satan in Eden, they create "relevance" by compromise, by side-stepping the inspiration of God—and, in so doing, they betray the truths of God that alone give the church authority and reason for existence.

The Bible, however, declares, "Where there is no revelation, the people cast off restraint" (Prov. 29:18). When churches compromise on moral questions of abortion, euthanasia, pre-marital and extra-marital sex, and homosexuality (as some churches are presently doing), they are themselves teaching the religion of Secular Humanism and must bear part of the responsibility for the deterioration of our society.

In spite of this, we do not despair. God's Word does work, and the church of Jesus Christ will remain. His grace always will sustain those whose confidence is in Him.

3. The School

The home and the church may be the institutions most vulnerable to subtle infiltration by the philosophy of secular humanism, but the school is the primary vehicle selected by Secular Humanists for direct spread of their doctrine.

Marilyn Ferguson (*The Aquarian Conspiracy*) and the Secular Humanists she quotes make it quite plain that they consider public education their eminent domain for the purpose of creating a wholly humanist society by the year 2000. In her zeal to turn public schools into humanist workshops, Ferguson obscures the truth and credits anything good in contemporary education to Secular Humanist educators. In truth, many of the Secular Humanist "discoveries" of the past few decades have been around a long time in Christian education: individualized instruction, special concern for every student (including care outside the classroom for those who needed special attention or support), the importance of attractive surroundings, stimulating activities, and curricula tailored to individual interest and competence. Simply stated, private and parochial schools must not be thought of as inferior to public schools; standard achievement tests quickly dispel that notion.

The above paragraph does not imply that every school in one system is superior to all schools in the other. The success of each school is dependent on the commitment of parents, school boards, administrators, and especially teachers to provide the best possible education for those entrusted to their care, sometimes at great personal sacrifice of time and energy.

More basic, however, than evaluating a school system's success is the underlying tenet that *parents* govern the education of their children. This means, first of all, that parents are to provide spiritual and moral training. Both the Old and New Testaments (e.g., Deut. 32:46–47 and Eph. 6:4) lay this imperative on the parents. Not that parents personally are to teach all the secular skills the child needs for life; rather, the parents' responsibility is to make certain that respect for God, "the beginning of wisdom" (Prov. 1:7), is maintained throughout the education of the child. This means personal involvement—including such things as participating in the selection of school board members, the formulation of school policy, the development of curricula, the approval of textbooks and reading materials, and the choice of administrators and teachers.

It also includes monitoring and evaluating what is happening in the school. For example, some administrators and teachers are seeking earnestly to deal with a lack of moral and personal responsibility in their students. In desperation, they may reach for any program that promises help, sometimes only to find that the philosophy behind the program is the philosophy partly responsible for the problems in the first place—situation ethics, self-centeredness, individual permissiveness instead of social responsibility, etc. These and other emphases have incurred the wrath of parents in many communities when they discovered that these programs contradicted and ridiculed the families' values and spiritual convictions, and replaced them with the opinions of Secular Humanist counselors and inexperienced peers.

The responsibility of Christians for public education is not limited to their own children, nor does it cease when they no longer have children of school age. Public education is what the name says: public. It must serve the whole community, without either the religion of Secular Humanism or denominational religious bias. In recent years, changes in public education have been brought about by citizens who were upset by what they saw as unfairness in other issues—racial or ethnic biases, lack of concern for children with special needs, etc. Similarly, Christian citizens have every right to raise questions of honesty and fairness if school curriculums omit or unfairly present information about the vital role religion has played in the history of the United States and the importance of religion in people's lives today. The suppression of facts also is a form of discrimination.

Christian citizens can make their concerns felt through curriculum committees, teachers and administrators, board members and the elective process, and parent-teacher organizations. Christians can approach these directly or through agencies that publicly represent their church bodies. The emphasis must not be on censorship but on 1) unbiased treatment of religious matters, and 2) what parents would like to see in the curriculum.

As an additional way for Christian citizens to support moral and spiritual education, parents may call for "released time" instruction under the auspices of local churches. With this arrangement, students attending public school are released for part of the day to attend religious instruction at church. This option has been upheld as constitutional by the Supreme Court (although Secular Humanists may not want to admit it). However, in order to be of value, such an arrangement must employ skilled teachers who relate the Word of God effectively, supporting the secular subjects taught in the public school. The reasons for this arrangement are fairness, choice, and professionalism in education, not the undermining of confidence in the public education system.

And, one additional option must be mentioned: private Christian schools. The importance of Christian education at all levels cannot be overstated. In addition to the basic requirements of mental and physical education, private Christian schools offer that which is not in the province of the public schools: "We speak not in the words taught by human wisdom but in words taught by the Spirit, expressing spiritual truths" (1 Cor. 2:13). Christian schools educate the whole person, both the horizontal and vertical dimensions. "Man does not live by bread alone but on every word that comes from the mouth of the Lord" (Deut. 8:3).

4. The Community

Christians need to "proclaim the truth in love" also in their communities, by what they do as well as by what they say—"that they may see your good deeds and praise your Father in heaven" (Matt. 5:16). Since the beginning of time, those who know their vertical, moral responsibility to God also know their responsibility to their fellow man. The question "Am I my brother's keeper?" was answered with the Creator's resounding "Yes!" (Gen. 4:9-10). And Saint Paul reminded believers of their "continuing debt to love one another, for he who loves his fellow man has fulfilled the law" (Rom. 13:8).

Humanist Marilyn Ferguson seems to think that concern for one's fellow man is another recent humanist discovery, at least from the political perspective. She quotes as an authority California governor Jerry Brown who called "mutual help in the private sector the first new idea to emerge in politics in twenty years" (*The Aquarian Conspiracy*, p. 216). Two hundred years of contributions by Christian Americans are dismissed as of no consequence.

In truth, many Christians and Secular Humanists share the same social concerns: starvation, suffering, disease, violence, ecological exploitation, pollution, crime, and war. Christians, however, may need to remind themselves that they are not to be so concerned with heaven that they ignore earthly concerns. Very clearly, one of the benefits of being re-created in Christ is that we are able "to do good works, which God prepared in advance for us to do" (Eph. 2:10). Imagine the tremendous moral and compassionate impact that could be made on contemporary society if all of America's professed Christians would exhibit in concrete ways their love of fellow man! Since more than ninety percent of Americans profess religious belief (the majority of these Christian), what sweeping moral and social changes would take place if their profession were translated into action!

Too quickly Christians sometimes say, "What difference can I make as only one person?" Or they sell themselves short of their God-given potential by asserting, "I can't do this or that," and then refuse to make the effort. Too often they fail to trust God for needed courage and resources and call it "humility." Christians need to remind themselves of the worth of all people: God values mankind so much he gave his only Son into death in order to redeem every person. Christians then need to confess, "I have been crucified with Christ and I no longer live, but Christ lives in me. The life I live in the body, I live by faith in the Son of God, who loved me and gave himself for me" (Gal. 2:20).

Ways in which Christian faith can be translated into action are limited only by one's imagination. They would certainly include, but not be restricted to:

Personal Spirituality
- Calling on the presence of God in daily, personal devotion and intercessory prayer;
- Worshiping regularly in a Christ-centered, confessional church and participating in organized Bible study;

A United Effort in the Church
- Striving for Bible-mandated position statements by their church on moral and social issues;
- Preparing for, entering, or serving in a vocation that is morally honorable and of benefit to fellow man;

Personal Sanctification
- Demonstrating the highest standards of speech, humor, and truth;
- Being a role model of Christian sexuality, whether married or single;
- Choosing friends and, as much as possible, associates whose demeanor strengthens and encourages moral conduct;
- Respecting the laws of the land for the common good and civil order;
- Managing their resources in a manner pleasing to God and protecting the property and rights of others;

Social Action
- Becoming involved personally in deeds of mercy or assistance as needs and opportunities arise;
- Supporting regularly church-related and secular charities;

Business Dealings
- Not bringing into the home anything that does not meet God's moral standards—literature, television programming, videos, and music;
- Refusing to patronize businesses and industries that sponsor offensive entertainment and stores that deal in offensive products;
- Supporting those businesses and industries that maintain high standards of decency in their sponsorships and advertising;
- Writing letters of commendation and encouragement to public figures, business leaders, corporations, and others who have maintained a strong moral position under pressure;

Community Involvement—Locally and At Large
- Conserving natural resources and doing what can be done to halt the scandalous waste and pollution that threaten our nation and world;
- Participating actively in parent-teacher organizations, school board meetings, and other community organizations;
- Running for school boards, youth councils, and the like, and nominating people who are morally sound as well as competent;
- Joining and supporting community and national organizations that stand for high moral ideals;
- Apprising elected representatives of their responsibility to God for their use of public trust;
- Voting, taking into consideration any moral issues involved and the candidate's position and record on those issues.

All of the above actions—and more—are part of the Christian's responsibility to God, and should be done without any smugness, fanaticism, self-aggrandizement, or malice. That which is valid and praiseworthy does not have to be offensive to be effective; it stands on its own merit.

Witness

The Holy Scriptures leave no doubt about it; the first and most effective response to Secular Humanism is the Christian's witness to the truth concerning what God has done for man in Jesus Christ. It is listed last here, not because it is "least," but for emphasis' sake; every response to Secular Humanism suggested in this book is motivated by the marvelous mercies of God.

The tragedy is that many who have come under the influence of Secular Humanism are not perpetrators but victims of its deception. Even if offended by Humanism's deification of fallible man, they have not been told of its dismal history of failure to improve the human condition. But, asks the Apostle Paul, "how can they believe in the one of whom they have not heard?" (Rom. 10:14).

The responsibility for making known the truth of God is laid at the feet of those who have experienced it. "In your hearts set apart Christ as Lord. Always be prepared to give an answer to everyone who asks you to give the reason for the hope that you have. But do this with gentleness and respect" (1 Pet. 3:15). Christian witness is, after all, "confession." That is, it is based on God's accomplishment in you through Jesus Christ. Christian witness is confessing one's dependence on God for life and sustenance. Christian witness is personally telling others God's truth—its power to bring into harmony all things, from the Christian's daily rejoicing in God's blessings to his eternal security in God's promises.

The frontiers of Christian missions (Mark 16:15) are found not only in pagan lands but in the "developed" lands as well, among "sophisticated" people. Because of Secular Humanism's growing influence, the most pagan street in the world could be the one on which your church is located, and the most pagan people those with whom you rub elbows daily. So honored are you, O Christian, that God has given you the role of being His spokesperson.

The Church of Jesus Christ is strong today in commitment even if not in numbers. Move among the people of God who are engaged in Bible study, prayer, and witness, and you will find that the Spirit of God is moving too.

Go, then, with the call "to give the reason for the hope that you have." Greater love you cannot show to God and your fellow man. Go with the mighty promise of God, "My word . . . will not return to me empty, but will accomplish what I desire and achieve the purpose for which I sent it" (Is. 55:11).

Recommended Reading

Lutzer, Erwin W., *Exploding the Myths That Could Destroy America*. Chicago: Moody Press, 1986.

Mains, David R., *The Rise of the Religion of Antichristism*. Grand Rapids: Zondervan, 1985.

Morey, Robert A., *The New Atheism and the Erosion of Freedom*. Minneapolis: Bethany House, 1986.

Overduin, Daniel, *Wake Up, Lucky Country!* Adelaide: Lutheran Publishing House, 1980.

From the Humanist point of view:

Humanist Manifestos I and II. Buffalo: Prometheus Books, 1977.

Ferguson, Marilyn, *The Aquarian Conspiracy*. Los Angeles: J. P. Tarcher, Inc., 1980.